Titles in Full Flight 7

Midsummer Mutants	David Orme
Beekeeper	Danny Pearson
Labyrinth	Melanie Joyce
The Incredible Save	Alison Hawes
Sci-Fi Spy Guy	Roger Hurn
Ghost Camp	Jillian Powell
Stone Beasts	Richard Taylor
Alien Speed Smash	Jonny Zucker
Jet Pack Power	Jonny Zucker
Hero: A War Dog's Tale	Jane A C West

Badger Publishing Limited
Suite G08, Business & Technology Centre
Bessemer Drive, Stevenage, Hertfordshire SG1 2DX
Telephone: 01438 791037   Fax: 01438 791036
www.badger-publishing.co.uk

Ghost Camp ISBN 978-1-84926-263-7

Badger Publishing would like to thank Jonny Zucker
for his help in putting this series together.

Publisher: David Jamieson
Editor: Danny Pearson
Design: Fiona Grant
Illustration: Mark Penman
Printed and bound in China through Colorcraft Ltd., Hong Kong

Contents

Badger Publishing

New words:

ouija board	shelter
gallows	energy
electrical	guess
drain	spinning
exploded	shudder
howling	map grids

Main characters:

Rashid

Ben

Eddie

Chapter 1
Stranded

"I am bored with this bus now!" Ben said. "Are we nearly there yet?"

"You sound like my kid brother!" Rashid told him.

"It's getting dark. How can we put tents up in the dark?" Eddie said.

Mr Smith turned round.

"Don't panic boys," he said. "We can't be far..."

The bus did a sudden jolt. The engine had died. Mr Smith got off with the driver. The driver shook his head.

"We're in the middle of nowhere. It's getting dark. The bus has died. We're stuffed!" Eddie said.

Mr Smith got back on. He was in a panic now.

"I'm sorry boys," he said. "We're stu..."

"Stuffed!" Eddie said.

"Stuck. We're stuck." Mr Smith said. "We're not going anywhere tonight. We'll have to sleep on the bus."

"NO way!" Rashid said.

"Sorry lads." Mr Smith said. "We'll get the bus fixed in the morning. It's just for tonight."

"Well I'm not sleeping on this bus!" Rashid said. "My back is killing me!"

"Can't we put the tents up?" Ben asked Mr Smith.

Mr Smith looked out of the bus.

"Well, yes, if you want," he said. "But it's not a campsite you know. It's just woods out there."

"It will be okay," Rashid said to Ben and Eddie. "It will be fun. Wild camping."

"We could try the tent out," Ben said.

"Yeah. Let's do it!" Eddie agreed.

The boys got off the bus, carrying their kit bags. The rest of the group seemed happy to stay.

"Idiots!" They heard someone say.

"Wimps!" Rashid replied.

Chapter 2

A Bad Place

"Here?" Eddie said. He threw down his kit bag.

"Don't be thick!" Rashid said. "Don't you know anything about camping? We need to be near water."

"Smithy said not to go too far," Ben pointed out.

The woods looked dark and a bit creepy.

"The woods will give us shelter and like I say, we need water. Come on!" Rashid said.

He led the way into the woods.

"Listen!" Ben said after a bit. "I can hear water over there."

"This will do," Rashid said. "Let's get this tent up before it gets too dark."

Ben and Eddie put the tent poles in while Rashid fixed the tent. It looked like a gale had gone through it. But at least it was up.

"Right, now we need some water," Rashid said.

The boys went up the hill with the water bottles.

"Hey look, that's weird," Ben said. "Water shouldn't do that!"

The boys stared at the water. It was running up hill.

"Well, as long as it's wet!" Eddie said. "Let's fill these up."

Ben got down and held his bottle in the water.

Then he jumped up yelling. "It's red. The water is turning red!"

It was true. It looked more like blood than water. The boys stared at each other. This place was creepy.

"Okay, forget the water. We'll use what we've got," Rashid said. "Let's get a fire going anyway."

They got some twigs and bits of dead wood to make a fire.

"I've done this before. There you go!" Rashid said as the fire began to burn.

Suddenly, orange flames exploded into the air.

The sky above them was thick and black. But it was not smoke. It was a mass of ravens. Their flapping wings and rough croaks filled the woods. A howling wind came with them, almost blowing the tent away.

Chapter 3

A Discovery

At last it was over.

"What on earth was that?" Ben said.

"I don't like it," Eddie said. "First the water. Now this. This place really is spooky."

He took out his phone.

"I thought so! The battery is low."

"So what?" Ben said. "You forgot to charge it up."

"I read this thing about ghosts needing energy to...well, to be ghosts," Eddie said. "They can drain mobile phones and stuff."

"That's stupid!" Ben said.

"Haven't you heard of those phone straps that bleep and flash when there's a ghost about?" Eddie said. "They've tested them in graveyards in Japan."

"We don't need one of those," Ben said.

He took out his phone. "I've got this app called GhostFinder. If there's anything strange going on, it will tell us."

"How?" Rashid said. "Is the ghost going to text you?"

Ben tapped the app.
"The software picks up tiny changes in the EMF," he explained.

"EMF?"

"Changes in the electrical field around us," Ben explained. "And if it picks anything up we will see it as ...Om-g."

"What? What?"

"Look at that!" Ben handed over his phone.

On the screen, a dial was spinning
round madly. Then it stopped. The dial
said "99.9% …100%. Ghost present."

"Look, this is mad. We are just getting
spooked," Rashid said. "Let's begin
with some facts, like where we are. I'll
check the GPS on my phone."

The others waited while he stared at
the map on the screen.

"That's it. Now if I zoom in, I can see…"

"Well?"

Rashid did a strange shudder. "This place. It's called Hangman Hill," he told them.

Chapter 4
Ouija

"Well that does it. This place gives me the creeps," Eddie said. "Let's go back to the bus."

"We can't do that, they'll think we're wimps," Rashid said. "Look, there are loads of places called Hangman Hill."

"Yeah, and it's where they hanged people. And just left them hanging until…"

"But all that was hundreds of years ago," Rashid said. "Look, I've got the map grids here. Let's do an internet search on this place."

"I'll try too," Ben said. "My phone is faster than yours."

They tapped in the map grids.

"See, I've got something already," Ben said. "It says there was a gallows here until 1860. And in 1814, the last person hanged was..."

"Hey, what's going on?" Rashid broke in. "Look, my phone wheel is going crazy..."

The wheel was spelling something out.
Letters were appearing on the screen.

"What's it saying?" Eddie said.

"W... I... L... L..."

"I think I can guess the rest." Ben was
staring at his own phone. "It says the
last person hanged here in 1814 was
a boy. He was 17 years old. And his
name was..."

"Will Cook."
Ben and Rashid
said together.

Chapter 5

A Goodbye

"I've read about this sort of thing," Eddie said. "The phone wheel works like a ouija board."

"Ask it something," Ben said. "Ask it what it wants to say."

They crowded round Rashid's phone.

Suddenly, the phone started to play a music track.

"What's that track?" Ben said.

"Why. Ask it why." Eddie said.

"He's talking to us.
Will Cook is talking
to us."

The phone went
silent. The boys
stared at each other.

"What do we do now?" Eddie said.

"He was telling us he didn't do it," Rashid said. "They made a terrible mistake when they hanged him."

"That's awful," Ben said. "He wasn't much older than us."

"He probably got hanged for something stupid like stealing a sheep or something. And he didn't even do it!"

"Tell him we believe him," Eddie said. "Tell him we're sorry."

Rashid tapped out the words.

"He doesn't even have a proper grave," Eddie said. "Let's get some stones and build something."

They found some stones and piled them up. Then they found some pinecones and spelled out his name: Will Cook.

"I've got this track on my phone, "We believe in you." Ben said. Let's play that."

"This is for you, Will Cook," they said. But Rashid's phone stayed silent.

Somehow, they slept. In the morning, Eddie woke the others.

"I've got some water!" He said. "It's running downhill and it's not red anymore."

"It feels different here somehow," Ben said. The stones and the pinecones were still in place.

Mr Smith had sent a text. The bus was mended and it was time to go.

"What do we tell them?" Eddie said.

"Nothing. They'll think we made it up," Rashid said.

As they reached the bus, Rashid's phone began to play a track.

"Everything worked out okay lads?"
Mr Smith asked. "Found a good place?"

"Found a bad place, left a good place!"
Rashid said.

"Idiots!" someone said from the back of
the bus.

Facts

- Before Victorian times (1837 - 1901) child criminals were punished in the same way as adults. They were sent to adult prisons, transported abroad, whipped and even sentenced to death for crimes including theft, shoplifting and arson.

- Children as young as 7 could be tried for crimes.

- The death sentence was still being used for children into the 1830s although by then the sentence was often reduced to imprisonment, hard labour or transportation.

- Public hangings for adults continued until 1868 and the death penalty was not finally abolished in England until 1965.

- 1814 5 children hanged at the Old Bailey, London: the youngest is 8 years old.

- 1838 Last year in which children receive death penalty.

The first juvenile prison opens

- 1847 The Juvenile Offences Act: young people under 14 (later 16) must be tried in a special court.

- 1854 The First Reformatory Schools set up for young offenders.

- 1868 The last public hanging.

- 1899 Children can no longer be sent to adult prisons.

- 1908 The Children's Act bans death penalty for children under 16.

Questions

- Why didn't Rashid want to spend the night on the bus?

- What did Rashid tell Ben and Mark they needed to camp near?

- What happened to the fire at the boy's campsite?

- What was the name of the ghost?

- What year did the death sentence stop in England?

- What would you have done if you found out there was a ghost at your campsite?